John Tappan Stoddard

An Outline of Qualitative Analysis

John Tappan Stoddard

An Outline of Qualitative Analysis

ISBN/EAN: 9783337139339

Printed in Europe, USA, Canada, Australia, Japan

Cover: Foto ©Andreas Hilbeck / pixelio.de

More available books at **www.hansebooks.com**

OF

QUALITATIVE ANALYSIS,

FOR BEGINNERS.

BY

JOHN T. STODDARD, PH. D.,

PROFESSOR OF CHEMISTRY IN SMITH COLLEGE.

Northampton, Mass.
Steam Press of Gazette Printing Company.
1883.

PREFACE.

The desire to place in the hands of my students who are beginning the study of Qualitative Analysis a clear, concise, and simple Outline of the subject, has led me to the preparation of this little work.

Much that is found even in elementary books is purposely omitted in this. Manipulation can only be satisfactorily learned from practical demonstration. Writing of equations and drawing up of analytical tables are valuable exercises for the student. Hence the little book presents only an OUTLINE, which is to be filled in by the student with the teacher's assistance.

The method which its arrangement suggests has been chosen as the one best calculated to give the student an intelligent grasp of the subject, and help him to become more than a mere analytical machine.

The student is expected to make all the reactions and express them in written equations. When this has been done for the members of a group of metals, a few solutions, each containing one or more members of the group, are given and analyzed according to the directions. The exercises on the group are then to be worked out. When each of the groups

has thus been thoroughly studied, a number of solids and solutions are given for systematic examination for all the groups.
These are at first of the simplest composition, and increase
gradually in complexity and analytical difficulty.

The detection of acids is now taken up in the same way,
except that an examination for metals, of course, always pre-
ceeds that for the acids.

Finally, a large variety of substances is given for complete
analysis.

J. T. S.

Smith College Laboratory.
      Dec. 25, 1882.

PART I.

DETECTION OF THE METALS.

SECTION I.

GROUPING OF THE METALS.

Group I. Metals which are precipitated as chlorides by HCl : Silver and Mercury (ous) completely, Lead incompletely.

Group II. Metals not falling under Group I, which are precipitated as sulphides from acid (HCl) solution by H_2S :—

Sub-group A : Sulphides insoluble in $(NH_4)_2S$: Mercury (ic), Lead, Bismuth, Copper, Cadmium.

Sub-group B : Sulphides soluble in $(NH_4)_2S$: Tin, Antimony, Arsenic, Gold, Platinum.

Group III. Metals not falling under Groups I and II, which are precipitated as hydroxides by NH_4OH in the presence of NH_4Cl : Iron, Chromium, Aluminium.

Group IV. Metals not falling under Groups I–III, which are precipitated as Sulphides by $(NH_4)_2S$: Nickel, Cobalt, Manganese, Zinc.

Group V. Metals not falling under Groups I–IV, which are precipitated as Carbonates by $(NH_4)_2CO_3$: Barium, Strontium, Calcium.

Group VI. Metals not falling under Groups I–V and having no common precipitant : Magnesium, Potassium, Sodium, Ammonium.

Group I.

REACTIONS.

Silver. Ag^t. Solution for reactions, AgNO$_3$.

1. HCl precipitates white curdy AgCl; soluble in NH$_4$OH, and in KCN; reprecipitated by HNO$_3$; darkens on exposure to light.

2. H$_2$S or (NH$_4$)$_2$S precipitates black Ag$_2$S; soluble in boiling HNO$_3$.

3. NH$_4$OH precipitates—from neutral solution only—brown Ag$_2$O; readily soluble in excess of NH$_4$OH.

4. NaOH precipitates brown Ag$_2$O.

5. K$_2$CrO$_4$ precipitates dark red Ag$_2$CrO$_4$; soluble in HNO$_3$ or in NH$_4$OH.

6. KI precipitates yellowish AgI.

7. Na$_2$HPO$_4$ precipitates yellow Ag$_3$PO$_4$.

8. Cu and some other metals precipitate metallic Ag.

9. (a) Heated with Na$_2$CO$_3$ on charcoal before the blowpipe, solid compounds of silver yield bright, malleable globules of Ag, (b) which are soluble in HNO$_3$.

Characteristic Reaction, 1.

Lead. Pb^{II}.   Solution for reactions, $Pb2NO_3$.

10. HCl precipitates (incompletely) white $PbCl_2$; soluble in boiling H_2O, and crystallizes from this solution on cooling; converted by NH_4OH into white $Pb.OH.Cl$, which is insoluble in H_2O.

11. H_2S or $(NH_4)_2S$ precipitates black PbS; soluble in hot HNO_3.

12. NH_4OH precipitates a white basic salt.

13. NaOH precipitates white $Pb(OH)_2$; soluble in excess.

14. K_2CrO_4 precipitates "chrome-yellow" $PbCrO_4$; soluble in NaOH; soluble with difficulty in HNO_3.

15. KI precipitates bright yellow PbI_2; soluble in boiling H_2O, and crystallizes from this solution, on cooling, in golden scales.

16. H_2SO_4 precipitates white $PbSO_4$; soluble in ammonium tartrate or NaOH.

17. Zn precipitates metallic Pb in crystalline form.

18. Compounds of Pb, heated with Na_2CO_3 on charcoal, yield soft, malleable, and easily fusible globules of Pb, and a yellow incrustation of PbO on the charcoal.   The globules are soluble in HNO_3.

Characteristic Reactions, 14, 15, 16.

Mercury. Hg_2^{II}.   *Mercurous Salts.*   Solution for reactions, Hg_22NO_3.

19. HCl precipitates white Hg_2Cl_2 (calomel); converted by NH_4OH into black NH_2Hg_2Cl.

20. H_2S or $(NH_4)_2S$ precipitates black Hg_2S; insoluble in hot HNO_3.

21. NH_4OH precipitates black $NH_2Hg_2NO_3$.

22. NaOH precipitates black Hg_2O ; decomposes readily into HgO and Hg.

23. K_2CrO_4 precipitates dark red basic chromate ; soluble with difficulty in HNO_3.

24. KI precipitates yellowish-green Hg_2I_2.

25. $SnCl_2$ precipitates grey Hg.

26. Cu and some other metals precipitate metallic Hg.

27. Compounds of Hg yield the metal readily when heated with Na_2CO_3 in a small tube. Hg is volatile and condenses on the cooler parts of the tube ; soluble in HNO_3.

Characteristic Reactions, 19, 27.

ANALYSIS.

(a) Add HCl until no further precipitation occurs; filter and wash with cold water. The *filtrate* may contain Groups II–VI. The white *precipitate* consists of one or more of the chlorides of Group I : AgCl, $PbCl_2$, Hg_2Cl_2.

(b) Add boiling H_2O to the precipitate on the filter (cf. 10). Test the filtrate for Pb by 10 and 14.

If Pb is found, the precipitate is washed repeatedly with hot water until free from it.

A residue insoluble in hot water indicates AgCl, Hg_2Cl_2, or both.

(c) Add NH_4OH ; Hg_2Cl_2 is blackened (cf. 19), while AgCl is dissolved (cf. 1), and its presence proved by adding HNO_3.

The black residue containing Hg is tested by 27.

EXERCISES.

I. Draw up a table for the analysis of this group.

II. Devise another method for the analysis of a solution containing the members of this group.

III. If $PbCl_2$ is not completely removed from the precipitate before adding NH_4OH, how is it affected by this reagent?

IV. Give the important compounds of the members of this group? Describe their appearance and uses.

Group II.

SUB-GROUP A.

Hg, Pb, Bi, Cu and Cd.

REACTIONS.

Mercury. Hg^{II}. *Mercuric Salts.* Solution for reactions, $HgCl_2$.

28. H_2S, added by degrees, produces, first, a white precipitate, which changes to orange, brownish red, and finally to black HgS. This is insoluble in hot HNO_3; soluble in aqua regia.

29. NH_4OH precipitates "white precipitate," NH_2HgCl.

30. $NaOH$ precipitates yellow HgO.

31. K_2CrO_4 precipitates an orange basic chromate; readily soluble in HNO_3.

32. KI precipitates yellow HgI_2, which rapidly becomes scarlet.

33. $SnCl_2$ precipitates white Hg_2Cl_2; if added in excess, grey metallic Hg.

34. Reactions 26 and 27 for mercurous salts.
Characteristic Reactions, 28 and 33.

Lead. Pb^{II}. PbS is precipitated by H_2S even from solutions of $PbCl_2$; so that lead belongs to both the first and second groups. Cf. reactions, 10–18.

Bismuth. Bi^{III}. Solution for reactions, $BiCl_3$.
35. H_2S precipitates black Bi_2S_3 ; soluble in HNO_3.
36. NH_4OH precipitates white BiO.OH ; becomes yellow Bi_2O_3 on boiling.
37. NaOH precipitates same.
38. K_2CrO_4 precipitates yellow $Bi_2 3CrO_4$; soluble in HNO_3 ; insoluble in NaOH.
39. Zn or Fe precipitates spongy Bi.
40. H_2O precipitates BiOCl ; insoluble in tartaric acid.
41. Heated on charcoal with Na_2CO_3, compounds of Bi yield hard, brittle globules, and a yellow volatile incrustation of Bi_2O_3. Bi is soluble in HNO_3 or aqua regia.
Characteristic Reactions, 40, 41.

Copper. Cu^{II}. Solution for reactions, $CuSO_4$.
42. H_2S precipitates black CuS ; soluble in HNO_3 and in KCN.
43. NH_4OH precipitates a greenish-blue basic salt, which dissolves in excess of NH_4OH, forming a dark blue solution.
44. NaOH precipitates pale blue $Cu(OH)_2$; converted by boiling into black CuO.
45. K_2CrO_4 precipitates a brownish-red basic chromate ; soluble in HNO_3 and in NH_4OH.

46. KCN precipitates greenish-yellow $Cu(CN)_2$; soluble in excess of KCN. H_2S produces no precipitate in this solution.

47. Fe or Zn precipitates metallic Cu. HCl aids the reaction.

48. Heated on charcoal with Na_2CO_3, compounds of Cu yield bright red, malleable particles without incrustation. Cu dissolves in HNO_3, and in conc. H_2SO_4.

Characteristic Reactions, 43 and 47.

Cadmium. Cd^{II}. Solution for reactions, $Cd2NO_3$.

49. H_2S precipitates yellow CdS; soluble in HNO_3; insoluble in KCN.

50. NH_4OH precipitates white $Cd(OH)_2$; soluble in excess.

51. NaOH precipitates the same.

52. K_2CrO_4 precipitates a yellow basic chromate; soluble in HNO_3.

53. KCN precipitates white $Cd(CN)_2$; soluble in excess and reprecipitated as CdS by H_2S. Cf. 46.

54. Zn precipitates Cd in brilliant scales.

55. Heated on charcoal with Na_2CO_3, compounds of Cd yield no metallic globules, but a brown incrustation of CdO. Cd dissolves readily in HNO_3.

Characteristic Reactions, 49 and 55.

PRECIPITATION OF GROUP II AND SEPARATION OF SUB-GROUPS A AND B.

(a) If the solution—or filtrate from Group I—contains free HNO_3, it must be evaporated with addition of HCl nearly to dryness. (b) Dilute with H_2O, and saturate the warm solution with H_2S. (c) Filter and wash with hot H_2O till free from HCl.

The *Filtrate* may contain Groups III–VI.

The *Precipitate* consists of some one or more of the sulphides of Group II : *A.* HgS, PbS, Bi_2S_3, CuS, CdS ; *B.* SnS, SnS_2, As_2S_3, Sb_2S_3.

(d) *Digest with warm, yellow $(NH_4)_2S_2$ for ten minutes. The sulphides of Sub-group B dissolve and are separated by filtration from the insoluble sulphides of Sub-group A. The latter are washed with hot H_2O till no longer alkaline.

Sub-Group A.—Analysis.

(e) The sulphides—HgS, PbS, Bi_2S_3, CuS, CdS— are boiled with a small quantity of strong HNO_3 ; the solution diluted and filtered :

(f) The *residue* may consist of HgS, black and heavy; $PbSO_4$, white and heavy ; Sulphur, light and floating. Dissolve HgS in aqua regia, expel excess of acid, and test with $SnCl_2$ (cf. 33).

(g) The *filtrate* may contain Pb, Bi, Cu, Cd. Add H_2SO_4 and filter if necessary.

White *precipitate*, $PbSO_4$. Dissolve in ammonium *NaOH* tartrate and test by 14.

(h) The *filtrate* may contain Bi, Cu, Cd. Add NH_4OH and filter if necessary.

White *precipitate*. Dissolve in a little conc. HCl ; expel excess of acid and pour into H_2O (cf. 40).

(i) *Filtrate* may contain Cu, Cd. If blue, Cu is present. Add KCN until the solution becomes color-

*In the absence of Sub-group B, omit this step and treat at once with HNO_3 as below (e).

2

less. Treat warmed solution with H_2S (avoid excess), yellow precipitate is CdS (cf. 53). If not blue, Cd alone can be present. Treat with H_2S.

EXERCISES.

V. Draw up a table for the analysis of this group.

VI. Why is the solution which is to be examined for Group II evaporated with HCl before treatment with H_2S (see a) ?

VII. Why is it important to wash the precipitated sulphides free from HCl (see c) ?

VIII. Explain the presence of S and that of $PbSO_4$ in the residue insoluble in HNO_3 (see f).

IX. If the filtrate from HgS (see g) were treated at once with NH_4OH, what would the precipitate contain, and how could it be examined ?

X. How may the color of the H_2S precipitate indicate the presence or absence of certain members of this group ?

XI. Give the important compounds of the members of this group ; their appearance and uses.

SUB-GROUP B : Sn, Sb and As.
REACTIONS.

Tin. a. Sn^{II}. *Stannous Salts.* Solution for reactions, $SnCl_2$.

56. H_2S precipitates dark brown SnS ; soluble in *yellow* $(NH_4)_2S_2$; reprecipitated as yellow SnS_2 by HCl.

57. NH_4OH precipitates white $Sn(OH)_2$.

58. NaOH precipitates same ; soluble in excess.

59. $HgCl_2$ precipitates white Hg_2Cl_2 (cf. 33).

60. Zn precipitates metallic Sn.

61. Heated on charcoal with Na_2CO_3 and borax, compounds of Sn yield white, malleable globules; in the oxidizing flame, slight white incrustation of SnO_2. Sn is soluble in conc. HCl; is converted by conc. HNO_3 into insoluble metastannic acid.

62. Stannous salts are converted into stannic by oxidizing agents: HNO_3, Cl, Fe_2Cl_6, etc.

b. Sn^{IV}. *Stannic Salts.* Solution for reactions, $SnCl_4$.

63. H_2S precipitates yellow SnS_2; soluble in $(NH_4)_2S$, in NaOH, and in hot conc. HCl.

64. NH_4OH precipitates white $SnO(OH)_2$.

65. NaOH precipitates the same; soluble in excess.

66. Reactions 60 and 61.

Characteristic Reactions; a. 56, 59; b. 63.

Antimony. Sb^{III}. Solution for reactions, $SbCl_3$.

67. H_2S precipitates orange Sb_2S_3; soluble in $(NH_4)_2S$, NaOH, and in hot conc. HCl.

68. NH_4OH precipitates white $Sb(OH)_3$.

69. NaOH precipitates same; soluble in excess.

70. H_2O precipitates from $SbCl_3$, white SbO.Cl; soluble in tartaric acid. Cf. 40.

71. Zn in presence of of HCl and Pt, precipitates Sb as a black powder, adhering to the Pt. The black stain on the Pt is not removed by HCl; but warm, conc. HNO_3 causes the stain to disappear by converting Sb into $HSbO_3$.

72. Heated on charcoal with Na_2CO_3, compounds of Sb yield a white incrustation of Sb_2O_3 and hard brittle globules of Sb, which are insoluble in HCl; oxidized by HNO_3; dissolved by aqua regia.

Arsenic. a. As^{III}. *Arsenious Compounds.* Solutions for reactions, Na_3AsO_3.

73. H_2S precipitates yellow As_2S_3; soluble in $(NH_4)_2S$ and in NaOH; reprecipitated by HCl; nearly insoluble in conc. HCl. Cf. 63 and 67.

74. NH_4OH and NaOH produce no precipitates.

75. $AgNO_3$ added to a neutral solution of an arsenite precipitates yellow Ag_3AsO_3.

76. $CuSO_4$ added to a neutral solution of an arsenite, precipitates $CuHAsO_3$, "Scheele's green."

77. Cu added to an HCl solution of arsenic becomes coated with a grey film of metallic As. *Reinsch's test.*

78. Arsenious compounds are converted by oxidizing agents into arsenic compounds. The simultaneous reduction of the oxidizing agent is shown in the following reactions: *a.* K_2CrO_4 warmed with arsenious compounds becomes green. *c.* $KMnO_4$ is decolorized.

b. As^V. *Arsenic Compounds.* Solution for reactions, Na_3AsO_4.

79. H_2S precipitates, in warm solutions free from HNO_3, As_2S_3 and S. Cf. 73.

80. Cf. 74.

81. $AgNO_3$, added to a neutral solution of an arsenate, precipitates reddish brown Ag_3AsO_4.

82. $MgSO_4$ precipitates, in the presence of NH_4OH and NH_4Cl, white crystalline $MgNH_4AsO_4$.

83. Heated on charcoal with Na_2CO_3, all compounds of arsenic are reduced to As, which volatilizes with a characteristic garlic odor.

84. Heated with charcoal in a glass tube, a "mirror" of metallic arsenic is obtained.

SUB-GROUP B—ANALYSIS.

(a) The sulphides SnS_2, Sb_2S_3, As_2S_3, are precipitated from the filtrate from Sub-group A by adding HCl to acid reaction. Filter and wash with hot H_2O. Boil with conc. HCl and filter.

(b) The *residue*, light yellow As_2S_3, is converted into a soluble arsenate by boiling with conc. HCl and a few crystals of $KClO_3$. Test by 82.

(c) The *filtrate* may contain Sn and Sb. Add Zn and platinum foil to the acid solution. Both metals, if present, are reduced to the metallic state, Sn being deposited on the Zn, and Sb as a black stain on the Pt. Remove excess of Zn, wash, add conc. HCl, warm to dissolve Sn, and filter.

(d) *Residue* is black ; Sb ; remove as far as possible from the Pt ; dissolve in aqua regia and expel excess of acid, dilute and test with H_2S.

(e) *Solution* may contain Sn ; expel excess of acid, dilute and test with $HgCl_2$.

Au and Pt belong to this Sub-group and in the course of analysis their sulphides, Au_2S_3 and PtS_2, being insoluble in HCl, remain in the residue with As_2S_3 (see b). By treatment with HCl and $KClO_3$, they are dissolved and detected by the following special tests :

Gold. Au[III.]
85. $SnCl_2 + SnCl_4$ produce a purplish coloration or precipitate ; " Purple of Cassius."
2*

Platinum. $Pt^{IV.}$

86. NH_4Cl precipitates yellow crystalline $2NH_4Cl$, $PtCl_4$; less soluble in alcohol than in H_2O.

EXERCISES.

XII. Draw up a table for the analysis of this group.

XIII. Devise another way for the detection of the members of this group, if in solution by themselves.

XIV. If H_2S were added to a solution containing all the members of Groups I and II, what would occur ?

XV. What is the action of $KClO_3$ in b ?

XVI. Give the important compounds of the members of this group; their appearance and uses.

Group III.

REACTIONS.

Iron. a. Fe^{II}. *Ferrous Salts.* Solution, $FeCl_2$.

87. $(NH_4)_2S$ precipitates black FeS; soluble in HCl.

88. NH_4OH or $NaOH$ precipitates white $Fe(OH)_2$, which quickly acquires a dirty green color, and ultimately becomes reddish brown $Fe_2(OH)_6$.

89. $(NH_4)_2CO_3$ or Na_2CO_3 precipitates white $FeCO_3$, which rapidly darkens in color.

90. $K_4Fe(CN)_6$ precipitates white $K_2Fe_2(CN)_6$, which rapidly becomes blue.

91. $K_3Fe(CN)_6$ precipitates "Turnbull's blue," $Fe_3Fe_2(CN)_{12}$.

92. KCNS produces no coloration.

93. Ferrous compounds are converted into ferric by oxidizing agents, such as (a)HNO_3, (b)$KClO_3$ and HCl, (c)Cl.

b. Fe^{IV}. *Ferric Salts.* Solution, Fe_2Cl_6.

94. $(NH_4)_2S$ precipitates black FeS and S.

95. NH_4OH, NaOH, $(NH_4)_2CO_3$, or Na_2CO_3 precipitates reddish brown $Fe_2(OH)_6$.

✓ 96. $K_4Fe(CN)_6$ precipitates "Prussian blue," $Fe_4Fe_3(CN)_{18}$.

✓ 97. $K_3Fe(CN)_6$ produces a reddish brown color.

98. KCNS produces an intense blood-red color.

99. Reducing agents, such as (a)H_2S, (b)SO_2, (c)$SnCl_2$, (d)As_2O_3, convert ferric into ferrous compounds.

100. Compounds of Fe color the borax bead ; yellowish red in the oxidizing flame ; green in the reducing flame.

101. Heated on charcoal with Na_2CO_3, compounds of Fe yield magnetic particles, but no globule.

Characteristic Reactions ; a. 91 ; b. 96 and 98.

Chromium. Cr^{IV}. a. *Chromium Salts.* Solution, $Cr_2 3SO_4$.

102. $(NH_4)_2S$ precipitates bluish green $Cr_2(OH)_6$; soluble in acids.

103. NH_4OH precipitates $Cr_2(OH)_6$.

104. NaOH precipitates $Cr_2(OH)_6$; soluble in excess ; reprecipitated by NH_4Cl or by boiling.

105. The oxide and salts of chromium are converted into chromic acid, or chromates, by powerful

oxidizing agents; c. g. fusion with Na_2CO_3 and KNO_3 on platinum foil gives yellow K_2CrO_4; soluble in H_2O.

b. *Chromic Acid.* Solution, K_2CrO_4.

106. Cf. 5, 14, 23, 31, 38, 45, 52.

107. Acids convert yellow K_2CrO_4 into red $K_2Cr_2O_7$; alkalies produce the reverse reaction, and *no precipitation.*

108. Reducing agents—(a)SO_2, (b)H_2S, (c) alcohol—convert solutions of chromates, to which HCl has been added, into green solutions of chrommium salts.

109. All compounds of chromium color the borax bead green.

Characteristic ; color of solutions and bead, 105.

Aluminium. Al^{IV}. Solution, $Al_2 3SO_4$.

110. $(NH_4)_2S$ precipitates white flocculent $Al_2(OH)_6$; soluble in acids.

111. NH_4OH precipitates the same.

112. NaOH precipitates the same ; soluble in excess ; reprecipitated by NH_4Cl.

113. Heated on charcoal, moistened with $Co2NO_3$ and heated again, compounds of Al yield an infusible blue mass.

Characteristic Reactions ; 112, 113.

(a) If the solution smells of H_2S (as will be the case if it is the filtrate from Group II), boil until all traces of this gas are expelled. If a ferrous salt (test a few drops by 91) is present, boil and add conc. HNO_3, a few drops at a time, till it is completely converted into a ferric salt. If the solution contains neither H_2S nor ferrous salts, begin at (b).

(b) Add to the hot solution NH_4Cl if the solution is to be examined for the following groups, and a slight excess of NH_4OH. Filter and wash with hot H_2O.

The *filtrate* may contain Groups IV–VI.

The *precipitate* consists of one or more of the hydroxides of Group III: $Fe_2(OH)_6$, $Cr_2(OH)_6$, $Al_2(OH)_6$.

(c) Dissolve the precipitate in HCl, add excess of NaOH and boil a few minutes; filter if necessary.

(d) The *precipitate* may contain Fe and Cr. Fuse on platinum foil with Na_2CO_3 and KNO_3; boil the mass, when cool, with H_2O, filter if necessary, boil the filtrate with acetic acid to expel CO_2, and test for Cr with $PbAc_2$. Cf. 14.

A *residue* insoluble in H_2O is dissolved in HCl and tested for Fe by 96 or 98.

(e) The *filtrate* may contain Al; acidify with HCl and add NH_4OH. Cf. 111.

EXERCISES.

XVII. Draw up a table for the analysis of this group.

XVIII. Describe the important compounds of the members of this group and their uses.

Group IV.

REACTIONS.

Manganese. $Mn^{II \text{ and } IV}$. Solution, $MnSO_4$.

114. $(NH_4)_2S$ precipitates flesh-colored MnS; soluble in acids, even in acetic acid.

115. NH_4OH precipitates (incompletely) whitish $Mn(OH)_2$, which soon darkens in color. In the presence of salts of ammonium this precipitate is not produced; but the solution, on standing, soon becomes cloudy, and ultimately all the Mn is precipitated as brown $Mn_2O_2(OH)_2$.

116. NaOH precipitates $Mn(OH)_2$.

117. Fused with Na_2CO_2 and KNO_3 on platinum foil, all compounds of Mn yield bright green Na_2MnO_4; soluble in cold H_2O, decomposed by boiling.

118. Compounds of Mn color the borax bead *amethyst* in the oxidizing flame.

Characteristic Reactions; 114, 117, 118.

Zinc. Zn^{II}. Solution, $ZnSO_4$.

119. $(NH_4)_2S$ precipitates white ZnS; soluble in HCl, but insoluble in acetic acid.

120. NH_4OH or NaOH precipitates white gelatinous $Zn(OH)_2$; soluble in excess of either reagent; reprecipitated from *dilute* solution by boiling, but not by NH_4Cl. Cf. 112.

121. Heated on charcoal with Na_2CO_3, compounds of Zn give an incrustation of ZnO, which is yellow while hot and white when cold.

122. Moistened with $Co2NO_3$ and strongly heated

before the blowpipe, compounds of Zn yield an infusible *green* mass.

Characteristic Reactions ; 119.

Cobalt. $Co^{II \text{ and } IV}$.   Solution, $Co2NO_3$.

123. $(NH_4)_2S$ precipitates black CoS ; insoluble in HCl ; soluble in HNO_3 and in aqua regia.

124. NH_4OH precipitates (incompletely) blue basic salts ; soluble in excess to a brownish red solution. Salts of ammonium prevent the precipitation.

125. NaOH precipitates the same ; converted by boiling into pale reddish $Co(OH)_2$. If exposed to the air without boiling, the precipitate turns green.

126. KNO_2 added to cobalt solutions, which are strongly acid with acetic acid, precipitate, on standing, a yellow crystalline double salt.

127. KCN precipitates brownish white $Co(CN)_2$; soluble in excess and reprecipitated by HCl or H_2SO_4. If to the solution in excess of KCN, a few drops of HCl be added and the solution boiled for some time, $6KCN, Co_2(CN)_6$ is formed, which is not precipitated by HCl or H_2SO_4, nor by NaClO.

128. Compounds of Co color the borax bead *deep blue.*

Nickel. $Ni^{II \text{ and } IV}$.   Solution, $Ni2NO_3$.

129. $(NH_4)_2S$ precipitates black NiS, slightly soluble in excess, forming a brown solution, from which it is reprecipitated by boiling ; insoluble in HCl ; soluble in HNO_3 or aqua regia.

130. NH_4OH precipitates (incompletely) light green $Ni(OH)_2$; soluble in excess, yielding a blue

solution.   Salts of ammonium prevent the precipitation.

131. NaOH precipitates the same.

132. KNO_2 in the presence of acetic acid produces no precipitate.

133. KCN precipitates yellowish green $Ni(CN)_2$; soluble in excess and reprecipitated by HCl or H_2SO_4, even after boiling. If the solution in excess of KCN be boiled with NaClO, black $Ni_2(OH)_6$ is precipitated. Cf. 127.

134. Compounds of Ni color the borax bead reddish brown in the oxidizing flame; grey in the reducing flame.

Characteristic Reactions ; 130, 131.

ANALYSIS.

(a) Add to the solution—or filtrate from Group III—$(NH_4)_2S$ till the precipitation is complete. Warm until the precipitate subsides ; filter and wash with hot H_2O to which a little $(NH_4)_2S$ has been added.

The *filtrate* may contain Groups V and VI. The *precipitate* consists of one or more of the sulphides of Group IV. If *light colored*, Co and Ni must be absent ; if *dark*, one or both of these metals is present.

I. All the group may be present.

Treat the precipitate with cold HCl. Filter and wash.

(b) The *residue* consists of CoS, NiS, or both. Test for Co with the borax bead (128). (1) If Co is *absent*, the bead shows the presence of Ni. Dissolve the residue in a small amount of aqua regia, expel excess of acid, dilute and confirm the presence of Ni by special reactions. (2) If Co is *present*, dissolve the residue in aqua regia, expel excess of acid, add a conc. solution of KNO_2 and acetic acid. After standing for several hours in a warm place the Co is all precipitated. Filter and test the filtrate for Ni by adding NaOH.

(c) The *filtrate* may contain $ZnCl_2$, $MnCl_2$, or both. Boil to expel H_2S, and add excess of NaOH. Cf. 116 and 120. A *precipitate* is $Mn(OH)_2$; filter and confirm the presence of Mn by 117. Test the filtrate for Zn by 119.

II. Co and Ni *absent*. Dissolve in HCl and examine the solution as in I. c.

EXERCISES.

XIX. Draw up a table for the analysis of this group.

XX. In what other ways can Ni be detected in the presence of Co ?

XXI. NH_4OH is added to an acid solution containing the members of the first four groups; what does the precipitate contain ? What change will the addition of an excess of NH_4OH produce ? How can the precipitate be examined ?

XXII. To a solution containing all of the third and fourth groups, $(NH_4)_2S$ is added ; of what does the precipitate consist ? How can it be analyzed ?

3

XXIII. A solution is known to contain Zn or Al, or both ; how is it to be examined ?

XXIV. Describe the important compounds of the members of this group and their uses.

Group V.

REACTIONS.

Barium. Ba^{II}. Solution, BaCl$_2$.

✓ 135. (NH$_4$)$_2$CO$_3$ or Na$_2$CO$_3$ precipitates white BaCO$_3$; soluble in acids, even in acetic acid.

136. Na$_2$HPO$_4$ precipitates white Ba$_2$HPO$_4$.

✓ 137. H$_2$SO$_4$, or a soluble sulphate, precipitates, even in dilute solutions, white BaSO$_4$; insoluble in acids.

138. CaSO$_4$ or SrSO$_4$ precipitates *immediately* BaSO$_4$.

139. K$_2$CrO$_4$ precipitates yellow BaCrO$_4$; soluble in HCl ; reprecipitated by NH$_4$OH ; insoluble in acetic acid.

140. H$_2$SiF$_6$ precipitates white BaSiF$_6$.

141. (NH$_4$)$_2$Ox precipitates white BaC$_2$O$_4$ from moderately strong solutions ; soluble in acetic acid.

142. Barium compounds give a yellowish green flame coloration.

Characteristic Reactions ; 137, 142.

Strontium. Sr^{II}. Solution, SrCl$_2$.

143. Cf. 135 and 136.

144. H$_2$SO$_4$ precipitates white SrSO$_4$; slightly soluble in H$_2$O, and hence does not appear at once in dilute solutions ; less insoluble in acids than BaSO$_4$.

145. $CaSO_4$ precipitates *slowly* on standing $SrSO_4$.

146. K_2CrO_4 precipitates, only in conc. solutions, yellow $SrCrO_4$. Presence of acetic acid prevents the precipitation.

147. H_2SiF_6 produces no precipitate.

148. $(NH_4)_2Ox$ precipitates white SrC_2O_4; soluble in HCl; only slightly soluble in acetic acid.

149. Strontium compounds produce a crimson flame coloration.

Characterictic Reactions; 145, 149.

Calcium. Ca^{II}. Solution, $CaCl_2$.

150. Cf. 135 and 136.

151. H_2SO_4 precipitates, from strong solutions, $CaSO_4$; less insoluble in H_2O and acids than $SrSO_4$.

152. $CaSO_4$, K_2CrO_4, and H_2SiF_6 give no precipitates.

153. $(NH_4)_2Ox$ precipitates white CaC_2O_4; soluble in HCl, but insoluble in acetic or oxalic acid.

154. Calcium compounds give a dull red flame coloration.

Characteristic Reactions; 153, 154.

ANALYSIS.

The solution—or filtrate from Group IV—if turbid or colored, is boiled till clear and filtered from deposited impurities. If acid, the solution must be rendered alkaline with NH_4OH. Add NH_4Cl and then precipitate by adding $(NH_4)_2CO_3$ to the warm solution. Filter and wash with hot H_2O.

The *filtrate* may contain Group VI.

The *precipitate* consists of one or more of the carbonates of Group V : $BaCO_3$, $SrCO_3$, $CaCO_3$. Dissolve in acetic acid.

Preliminary test. To a small portion of the solution in HAc, add $CaSO_4$ solution. An immediate precipitate indicates that Ba is, and Sr and Ca may be present (I). A precipitate after some time shows that Ba is absent, but Sr is and Ca may be present (II). No precipitate indicates that Ba and Sr are absent and that Ca alone is present (III).

I. *All the Group may be present.* Add to the HAc solution, K_2CrO_4 in slight excess and filter. The *precipitate* is $BaCrO_4$; dissolve in HCl and test by 137 and 142.

The *filtrate* is made alkaline with NH_4OH and $(NH_4)_2CO_3$ added. A *precipitate* is $SrCO_3$, $CaCO_3$, or both ; wash till white and dissolve in HAc. Test a small portion of this solution for **Sr** by adding $CaSO_4$ solution, or by the flame reaction (149). (a) If Sr is present, add a dilute solution of $(NH_4)_2SO_4$. After standing for some time, filter from the *precipitated* $SrSO_4$ and test the *filtrate* for Ca by adding NH_4OH and $(NH_4)_2Ox$ (153). (b) If Sr is absent, test at once for Ca by 153.

II. *Ba absent, Sr present.* Proceed as in I, a.
III. *Ba and Sr absent.* Test for Ca by 153.

Group VI.

REACTIONS.

Magnesium. Mg^{II}. Solution, $MgSO_4$.
155. NH_4OH and $(NH_4)_2CO_3$ give no precipitates in the presence of salts of ammonium.

156. Na_2HPO_4 produces, in the presence of NH_4OH and NH_4Cl, a white crystalline precipitate of $MgNH_4PO_4$. The precipitation is slow in dilute solutions ; but is hastened by warming and agitation.

157. H_2SO_4, H_2SiF_6 and $(NH_4)_2Ox$ produce no precipitates.

158. Ignited on charcoal, compounds of Mg yield an infusible luminous mass, which, on being moistened with $Co2NO_3$ and again ignited, assumes a *pale rose* color.

Characteristic ; 156, 158.

Potassium. K^I. Solution for reactions, KCl.

159. $PtCl_4$ precipitates, except in very dilute solutions, yellow crystalline $PtCl_4,2KCl$; insoluble in alcohol.

160. NaHTr or H_2Tr precipitates white crystalline KHTr from concentrated solutions.

161. H_2SiF_6 precipitates white gelatinous K_2SiF_6.

162. Potassium compounds color the flame *violet*, appearing reddish-violet through blue glass.

Characteristic ; 162.

Ammonium. NH_4^I. Solution, NH_4Cl.

163. $PtCl_4$ precipitates yellow crystalline $PtCl_4,2NH_4Cl$; insoluble in alcohol. On ignition, the precipitate leaves a residue of spongy platinum.

164. NaHTr or H_2Tr precipitates white crystalline NH_4HTr from concentrated solutions.

165. H_2SiF_6 gives no precipitate.

166. *Nessler's solution* produces a brown precipi-

3*

tate, or in very dilute solutions a brownish-yellow coloration.

167. Heated with NaOH, compounds of NH_4 evolve NH_3, which is recognized by its odor, alkaline reaction and fuming with HCl.

168. Heated on platinum, compounds of NH_4 volatilize completely.

Sodium. Na^i. Solution for reactions, NaCl.

169. $PtCl_4$, NaHTr and H_2Tr, give no precipitates.

170. H_2SiF_6 precipitates white gelatinous Na_2SiF_6.

171. Sodium compounds produce an intense yellow flame coloration, which is not visible through blue glass. A crystal of $K_2Cr_2O_7$ appears colorless when illuminated by the sodium flame. .

ANALYSIS.

The solution—or filtrate from Group V—is concentrated by evaporation and a portion ignited on platinum foil. If *no residue* is left, Mg, K and Na are absent. Test the original solution or substance for NH_4 by 167.

If a *residue is left*, Mg, K, Na may be present. Test a small portion of the concentrated solution for Mg by 156, and then proceed with the examination for K and Na by I or by II according to the result.

I. *Mg is present.* (a) Employ the flame tests, 162 and 171. A strong sodium flame masks a potassium flame ; but blue glass cuts off the yellow and allows the detection of K in the presence of Na.

Or (b), evaporate the solution to dryness, ignite the residue to expel salts of NH_4, dissolve it in a little H_2O, and add $Ba(OH)_2$ to alkaline reaction ; boil, filter ; The precipitate is $Mg(OH)_2$. The *filtrate* contains Na and K, if present, as hydroxides, and the excess of $Ba(OH)_2$; precipitate the Ba with $(NH_4)_2CO_3$, filter and evaporate the filtrate to dryness and ignite. The residue can now contain only Na, K. Test for K by 159, or 160 ; for Na by 171.

II. *Mg is absent.* Evaporate the concentrated solution and ignite ; dissolve the residue in a little H_2O and test for K and Na as in I. b.

A special test for NH_4 is always made by heating a portion of the original substance or solution with NaOH (cf. 167).

EXERCISES.

XXV. Draw up tables for the analysis of Groups V and VI.

XXVI. Give as many ways as possible for detecting K in the presence of Na.

XXVII. Devise other ways for analyzing this group.

XXVIII. Describe the important compounds of the members of Groups V and VI and give their uses.

SECTION III.

Chapter I.

PRELIMINARY EXAMINATION.

A. The Substance is a Solid.

I. *A portion of the powdered substance is heated in a glass tube sealed at one end.*

a. *Water* condenses on the cool part of the tube. This may indicate (1) adherent or enclosed (decrepitation) H_2O. (2) Salts containing H_2O of crystallization (fusion followed by solidification). (3) Decomposable hydrates. The water may be alkaline or acid, and thus indicate the presence of NH_4 or a volatile acid.

b. *Gases or fumes* are given off.

1. NO_2 recognized by its color and odor, indicates nitrates or nitrites.

2. Cl_2, Br_2 or I_2,—color and odor ; certain chlorides, bromides or iodides.

3. NH_3—odor, fumes with HCl ; salts of NH_4.

4. SO_2—odor ; sulphate or sulphite.

5. H_2S—odor ; hydrated sulphides.

6. CN—odor, crimson flame ; certain cyanides.

7. CO_2 extinguishes a match, renders a drop of lime water turbid ; carbonates and oxalates.

8. CO burns with blue flame ; oxalates.

9. O_2 rekindles spark ; chlorates, nitrates or per-oxides.

10. N_2O rekindles spark ; NH_4NO_3 or other nitrate with a salt of NH_4.

c. *A sublimate* is formed. If *white*, it may be :—

1. Salts of NH_4 ; heated with NaOH yield NH_3.

2. Chlorides of Mercury ; (a) Hg_2Cl_2 sublimes without fusion ; is yellow while hot and white when cool. (b) $HgCl_2$ fuses before it sublimes.

3. As_2O_3 ; crystalline, gives As mirror when heated with charcoal in a glass tube.

4. Sb_2O_3 melts and sublimes in needles.

5. Certain organic acids.

If *yellow*, it may be :—

6. S ; sublimes in reddish brown drops, which turn yellow on cooling ; sulphur or certain sulphides.

7. As_2S_3 ; reddish while hot, yellow when cool.

8. HgI_2 ; turns red when rubbed.

If *dark* or of *metallic lustre*, it may be :—

9. I_2 ; feathery and black. Cf. **b. 2**.

10. HgS ; black, becomes red when rubbed.

11. Hg ; grey mirror, white globules when rubbed.

d. *The substance or residue changes color.* 1. If the substance blackens it may be from the formation of a black oxide, or from the charring of organic matter. In the latter case smoky fumes and tar are usually evolved ; acetates give the odor of acetone ; tartrates the odor of burnt sugar ; organic salts of the alkalies and alkaline earths yield carbonates which effervesce with acids.

2. The residue shows one of the following changes :

Yellow	while hot,	white	when cold ;	ZnO.
Yellow brown	" "	yellow	" "	SnO_2.
Red brown	" "	pale yellow	" "	Bi_2O_3.
Red brown	" "	yellow	" "	PbO.
Black	" "	red	" "	Fe_2O_3.

e. *The substance fuses without decomposition or sublimation.* Salts of the alkalies and certain salts of the alkaline earths (nitrates, chlorides, etc).

II. *A small portion is heated on charcoal before the blowpipe.*

1. The substance deflagrates ; nitrates or chlorates.
2. It melts and runs into the charcoal ; salts of the alkalies and some salts of the alkaline earths.
3. It gives off SO_2 ; sulphur or sulphides.
4. It volatilizes ; cf. I. c.
5. It gives a coating on the charcoal ; cf. III. b.
6. An infusible white residue remains. Moisten with $Co2NO$ and ignite ; a blue color indicates Al, SiO_2, or phosphates ; green, Zn : pink or rose, Mg.

III. *A small portion of the finely powdered substance is mixed with Na_2CO_3 and heated on charcoal in the inner blowpipe flame (reduction).*

a. *Metallic globules* or particles are obtained *without a coating* on the charcoal. Ag, Cu, Au yield globules ; Pt, Fe, Co, Ni yield no globules, but infusible metallic particles, all of which except Pt are *magnetic*.

b. *A coating on the charcoal* is produced, with or

without the formation of a metallic bead. The coating is :—

1. White, very volatile, emitting a garlic odor ; no globule ; As.

2. White, less volatile than (1) ; globules usually formed, which are brittle and hard ; Sb.

3. Yellow while hot, turns white on cooling, close to the substance, no globules ; Zn.

4. Pale yellow while hot, white on cooling, non-volatile ; globules formed with difficulty, which are malleable and readily fusible ; Sn.

5. Lemon yellow, volatile; globules readily formed, easily fusible, soft and malleable ; Pb.

6. Orange yellow while hot, becomes lemon yellow on cooling, volatile ; globules hard and brittle ; Bi.

7. Reddish-brown and volatile ; no globule ; Cd.

c. *The fused mass is removed from the charcoal and crushed on a silver coin with a drop of water.*

The silver is stained brown or black (Ag_2S) ; sulphides or sulphates in the original substance.

IV. *A small portion is fused in a borax bead formed in a loop of platinum wire.*

BORAX BEADS.

Outer Flame.		Metal.	Inner Flame.
HOT.	COLD.		
Green.	Green.	Cr.	Green.
Green.	Blue.	Cu.	Opaque and reddish.
Blue.	Blue.	Co.	Blue.
Violet.	Brown.	Ni.	Grey and cloudy.
Violet.	Amethyst.	Mn.	Almost colorless.
Red.	Yellow.	Fe.	Bottle green.

V. *A clean platinum wire is moistened with HCl, dipped into the powdered substance and held in the edge of the Bunsen flame.* The flame is colored

  1. Yellow, not visible through blue glass; Na.
  2. Violet, reddish violet through blue glass; K.
  3. Crimson, Sr.
  4. Orange red ; Ca.
  5. Green ; H_3BO_3.
  6. Yellowish green ; Ba.
  7. Blue changing to green ; Cu.

VI. *If the substance is not a metal, a small portion is mixed with conc. H_2SO_4 in a dry test tube and the mixture carefully heated, if a reaction does not take place in the cold.*

  a. The following gases may be evolved :—
HCl, $HBr+Br_2$, I_2, HF, HCN, HNO_3 HAc, from their respective salts ; (HF is partially converted into SiF_4, which renders turbid a drop of H_2O on the end of a glass rod) ; CO_2 from carbonates ; SO_2 from sulphites or thiosulphates or by tartrates ; NO_2 from nitrites ; H_2S from sulphides ; O_2 from peroxides, chromates (turn green), permanganates (become colorless) ; CO from oxalates or ferrocyanides ; Cl from hypochlorites ; Cl_2O_4 from Chlorates.

  b. Blackening of the mixture indicates organic matter.

VII. *After finishing the preliminary examination, treat the substance with solvents.* See chap. II. p. 34.

B. The Substance is a Liquid.

I. *A few drops are carefully evaporated on platinum foil to dryness.*

a. No residue remains ; H_2O and some other volatile liquids.

b. A residue remains ;
1. Which disappears on ignition ; compounds of NH_4, Hg, As, Sb or certain organic acids. Cf. A. I. c.
2. Which changes color. Cf. A. I. d.
3. Which fuses without volatilizing. **Cf. A. I. e.**
4. Which *may* be further examined by **A. II–VI.**

II. *Test with Litmus paper (blue and red).*

a. The solution is neutral ; only a few salts can be present, chiefly chlorides, nitrates, and sulphates of the alkalies or alkaline earths.

b. The solution is acid. It may contain : (1) a free acid or acid salt, (2) a normal salt with acid reaction. In the first case a drop of Na_2CO_3 solution gives no permanent precipitate ; in the second, the turbidity or precipitate usually remains.

c. The solution is alkaline. This indicates the presence of hydroxides, sulphides, or certain salts of the alkalies or alkaline earths.

III. Proceed to the analysis by chap. III.

4

Chapter II.

SOLUTION OF SOLIDS.

A. The Substance is neither a Metal nor an Alloy.

I. *Add some water* to a small quantity of the finely powdered substance in a test tube; heat, and finally boil if necessary.

a. *Complete solution takes place.* Dissolve a larger portion sufficient for analysis, and after examining the solution with test-papers (cf. chap. I. B. II.), proceed with the examination according to chap. III.

b. *If a considerable residue* remains undissolved, it is usually best to consider the substance insoluble in water, and proceed according to II. Whether partial solution has taken place or not can be ascertained by filtration and evaporation on platinum foil (cf. chap. II. B. I). *If the residue is quite small,* it is well to filter and treat the solution according to chap. III; the residue according to B.

c. Soluble in water are :—All nitrates, chlorates and hypochlorites; nitrites ($AgNO_2$ *sparingly*); acetates ($AgAc$ and Hg_2Ac_2 *sparingly*); sulphates *except those of Ba, Sr, Ca, Pb*; chlorides, bromides and iodides *except those of Ag, Hg_2, (Pb)*; the borates, carbonates, oxalates, phosphates and sulphites of the alkalies; the oxides, hydroxides, sulphides, cyanides, ferrocyanides and ferricyanides of the alkalies and alkaline earths; the fluorides of the alkalies and of Ag, Sn, Hg, Bi, Sb, Al, Cr and Fe^{IV}.

II. *Substances insoluble in water* are treated with acids in the following order, till they dissolve or prove to be insoluble in all acids : HCl, HNO_3, aqua regia. The acid used is first dilute, then concentrated ; and in each case is heated before passing to the next. If solution takes place, proceed according to chap. III, if not, see III. It is important to *avoid using an excess of acid*, especially if HNO_3 or aqua regia is the solvent.

III. *Substances insoluble in water and acids.* The most common are : sulphates of Ba, Sr, (Ca), Pb ; AgCl, AgBr, AgI, AgCN, CaF_2 ; ignited Al_2O_3, Fe_2O_3, Cr_2O_3 ; SnO_2 ; SiO_2 and many silicates ; certain ferrocyanides and ferricyanides ; S and C.

The preliminary examination gives a clue to the composition of most of these. C is black and infusible, but disappears when ignited on platinum foil (graphite and gas carbon are scarcely affected) ; deflagrates when heated with KNO_3. SiO_2 and silicates swim undissolved in a bead of microcosmic salt.

(1) *Silicates* are mixed with four times the quantity of $K_2CO_3 + Na_2CO_3$ and fused in a platinum crucible. When cool add H_2O and a little HCl and evaporate to dryness. On treating the residue with H_2O, silica remains undissolved, while the metals, which were originally present as silicates, go into solution as chlorides. If an insoluble silicate is to be examined for Group VI, fuse with $Ba(OH)_2$, or dissolve in HF.

(2) *Sulphates of Ba, Sr, Ca,* and Al_2O_3, Fe_2O_3 are fused as in 1 ; the fused mass is washed with

H_2O as long as anything dissolves ; filter and dissolve the residue in HCl.

(3) $PbSO_4$ may be dissolved in ammonium tartrate ; AgCl, AgBr, AgI and AgCN may be dissolved in KCN or reduced by $Zn + H_2SO_4$.

(4) CaF_2 is decomposed by conc. H_2SO_4 in a platinum or lead dish.

(5) SnO_2 is fused in a porcelain crucible with equal parts of Na_2CO_3 and S. The fused mass is extracted with H_2O and SnS_2 prec. by HCl.

(6) *Insoluble compounds of Cr* are fused in a platinum crucible with equal parts of Na_2CO_3 and KNO_3. Boiling H_2O dissolves from the mass K_2CrO_4. A residue insoluble in H_2O is dissolved in HCl.

(7) *Ferrocyanides and ferricyanides* are decomposed by boiling NaOH into ferrocyanides and ferricyanides of Na soluble in H_2O, and hydrates of the metals soluble in acids.

After a solution is obtained it is examined according to chap. III.

B. The Substance is a Metal or an Alloy.

It is treated with HNO_3, and boiled if necessary :

a. *Complete solution* takes place.   Au, Pt, Sb and Sn are absent.

b. *A residue* is left ; (a) if *metallic :* Au, Pt ; dissolve in aqua regia.   (b) Residue is *white :* Sb, Sn, or certain nitrates sparingly soluble in HNO_3. Treat with H_2O ; the nitrates dissolve ; to a residue, add hot conc. H_2Tr ; Sb dissolves and is tested with H_2S ; Sn remains undissolved and may be treated by III, 5.

Chapter III.

EXAMINATION OF SOLUTIONS FOR METALS.

a. `Add to the solution a few drops of HCl or enough to render it distinctly acid, if originally alkaline. A precipitate shows the presence of *Group I* (cf. g); see p. 5, Analysis.

b. To a *small test* of the solution in which HCl has failed to produce a precipitate, or of the filtrate from Group I, add H_2S until the odor is distinct after shaking and warming gently. If no precipitate or turbidity is produced, pass to c. If H_2S causes a precipitate or turbidity, add the test to the solution and treat the whole with H_2S (cf. h); see p. 8, Precipitation of *Group II*, and pp. 9 and 13, Analysis.

c. To a fresh test of the original solution, or to a test of the filtrate from Group II from which H_2S has been expelled by boiling and which contains no ferrous Fe (cf. p. 16, Analysis), add NH_4Cl and NH_4OH. If no precipitate is formed, pass to d. A precipitate shows the presence of *Group III* (cf. i); see p. 16, Analysis.

d. To the test in which NH_4OH procured no precipitate, or to a test of the filtrate from Group III, add $(NH_4)_2S$. If no precipitation takes place, pass to e. A precipitate shows the presence of *Group IV;* see p. 20, Analysis.

e. To the test which NH_4OH and $(NH_4)_2S$ failed to precipitate, or to a test of the filtrate from Group IV, add $(NH_4)_2CO_3$. A precipitate shows the pres-

4*

ence of *Group V;* see p. 23, Analysis. If no precipitate is formed, examine the solution or filtrate for *Group VI* according to p. 26, Analysis.

Notes on the precipitation and separation of Groups.

f. When a group is found to be present, the group reagent must be added till it is *completely* precipitated. This is the case, if, after thorough agitation, addition of another drop of the reagent produces no precipitate, or the solution smells of the reagent. At the same time a large excess of the reagent is to be avoided. The precipitates must be *thoroughly washed* to free them from adhering solution which may contain the succeeding groups.

g. *Group I.* If the solution is alkaline, HCl may precipitate As_2S_3, Sb_2S_3, SnS_2 (cf. p. 13, a) ; cyanides dissolved in KCN ; gelatinous $(HO)_4Si$; or S from alkaline sulphides. HCl may also cause the evolution of CO_2, H_2S, SO_2,—sometimes attended by separation of S, or HCN (cf. p. 32, VI, a). SbOCl and BiOCl are sometimes precipitated at first by *dilute* HCl, but dissolve when more acid is added.

h. *Group II.* The solution into which H_2S is led must not be strongly acid even with HCl, as in this case the sulphides of the group—especially CdS— are not readily precipitated. The difficulty may be corrected by dilution or evaporation. At the same time the solution must be sufficiently acid to prevent partial precipitation of ZnS. Turbidity on dilution indicates the presence of Bi or Sb (cf. 40 and 70).

i. *Group III.* The precipitate almost always contains some Mn when this is present in the solution under examination. Its presence is shown by the green color of the mass obtained in testing for Cr. The green manganate is decomposed on boiling with H_2O and Cr is detected in the usual way in the filtrate. cf. p. 17, d.

j. On account of the imperfect separation of Groups III and IV by means of NH_4Cl and NH_4OH, it is in some cases best to precipitate both groups by $(NH_4)_2S$. HCl dissolves all but CoS and NiS. The filtrate is freed from H_2S; ferrous Fe, if present, is oxidized by HCl and $KClO_3$, and the solution when cold is treated with $BaCO_3$. After shaking several times during twenty minutes, filter and wash. The precipitate contains hydroxides of Fe, Cr and Al, and excess of $BaCO_3$; the filtrate Zn, Mn and $BaCl_2$.

k. The precipitate produced by NH_4OH may contain or consist of phosphates or oxalates of the alkaline earths, as these substances are only soluble in *acid solutions*. They need not be looked for if the original substance was soluble in H_2O, or if the original solution was alkaline. Tests for phosphoric and oxalic acids should, however, be at once made (a) when a precipitate for Group III is obtained which further examination shows to contain none of the groups; (b) or when a precipitate is obtained for Group III, and none for Group V or Mg, although the Preliminary Examination has indicated the presence of one or more of these metals.

(1) If an oxalate is detected, a portion of the original substance is *ignited*. The oxalate is thus converted into a carbonate which is dissolved in HCl and examined in the usual way.

(2) If a phosphate is present, add to the Group III precipitate a considerable quantity of metallic tin and conc. HNO_3. Heat until all the tin is oxidized. Phosphate of tin, insoluble in HNO_3 is thus formed. Dilute with H_2O, filter and examine the filtrate, which contains the nitrates of the metals originally present as phosphates, in the usual way.

EXERCISES.

XXIX. Name the most important metals and alloys and their uses.

XXX. On adding the reagent for Group II to a solution, no precipitate is formed, but the solution becomes turbid ; to what may this be due ?

XXXI. Chromates give no precipitate with NH_4OH ; how then is Cr detected in the ordinary course of analysis when present in the original solution as chromate ?

XXXII. A solution containing Fe, Al, Co, Cu, Zn, Mn and free acetic acid is treated with H_2S ; what precipitation, if any, takes place ?

XXXIII. A solution contains members of Groups II, III, IV and V : (a) The precipitation by H_2S is *incomplete*; how may this affect the examination of the following groups ? (b) The precipitate formed by H_2S is complete but is *insufficiently washed;* what difficulties may arise in its examination ?

XXXIV. Solutions of Bi and Sb are both precipitated by H_2O ; how can the precipitates be distinguished ?

XXXV. Why must H_2S be expelled from the filtrate of Group II before boiling with HNO_3 ?

XXXVI. How may the examination of a solution be simplified if it is known that it contains but one metal ?

XXXVII. How are the precipitate and filtrate obtained in the method of separating Groups III and IV by $BaCO_3$ (cf. p. 39, j), to be further examined ?

XXXVIII. A solution contains Al, Ni, Mn, Zn and free HCl. After the addition of a certain reagent, H_2S precipitates ZnS alone from the solution. What is the reagent employed ?

XXXIX. The filtrate from Group IV is often brown. What is the reason of this ? How can the color be removed ?

XL. How can a ferrous salt be detected in the presence of a ferric compound ?

XLI. How is bismuth chromate distinguished from lead chromate ?

XLII. NaOH is added in excess to a solution containing members of the first four groups; of what may the precipitate consist ? What change will be produced by boiling ?

XLIII. H_2SO_4 is added to the filtrate from Group I ; of what may the precipitate consist ?

PART II.

DETECTION OF THE ACIDS.

SECTION I.

REACTIONS OF THE ACIDS.

Group I.

ACIDS WHICH ARE PRECIPITATED FROM NEUTRAL
SOLUTIONS BY $BaCl_2$.

Sub-group A: *Acids whose Barium salts are insoluble in HCl:*—H_2SO_4, (H_2SiF_6).

Sulphuric Acid and Sulphates. See Reactions **137**, 16 and p. 31, **c**.

172. *Free* H_2SO_4 may be detected by putting a few drops of the solution on writing paper and gently warming. The acid, if present, will be concentrated and blacken the paper.

Hydrofluo-silicic Acid and Silico-fluorides. See Reactions 140, 161, 170. Solid silico-fluorides heated with conc. sulphuric acid give HF, which fumes and etches glass, and fluoride of silicon.

Sub-group B: *Acids whose Barium Salts are soluble in HCl:*—H_3PO_4, H_2CO_3, HF, $(HO)_4Si$, $(HO)_3B$, H_2Ox, H_2Tr, H_2CrO_4, H_3AsO_4, H_3AsO_3, $(H_2SO_3, H_2S_2O_3)$.

Phosphoric Acid and Phosphates. See Reactions 7, 136, **156.**

173. If a few drops of a solution containing phosphoric acid or a phosphate be added to a solution of ammonium molybdate in HNO_3, a pale yellow precipitate of ammonium phosphomolybdate is produced.

Carbonic Acid and Carbonates. See Reaction 135.

174. HCl and all other free acids—except HCN and H_2S—decompose carbonates, usually with evolution of CO_2—effervescence—which renders lime water turbid. The effervescence *always* occurs when the acid is in *excess*—as when the carbonate is added to the acid.

Heat converts many carbonates into oxides.

Hydrofluoric Acid and Fluorides. BaF_2 is white and soluble in HCl.

175. Heated with conc. H_2SO_4, all fluorides are decomposed with evolution of HF, which fumes and etches glass. If the fluoride contains much SiO_2, or if the decomposition takes place in a glass vessel, SiF_4 is formed, which is recognized by causing turbidity in a drop of H_2O.

176. Heated with $KHSO_4$ in a borax bead, BF_3 is formed, which colors the flame green.

Silicic Acid and Silicates.

177. All silicates, except those of the alkalies are insoluble in H_2O. HCl added drop by drop to a strong solution of a silicate, precipitates gelatinous silicic acid ; but if added to a dilute solution or in large excess, no precipitate is formed. Some silicates are decomposed by acids—HCl or H_2SO_4,—others must be fused with Na_2CO_3 (see p. 35, 1). In either case, evaporation with an acid to dryness must follow the decomposition, in order to render the silica insoluble.

178. Ba_2SiO_4 is decomposed by HCl with separation of gelatinous $(HO)_4Si$.

179. All silicates dissolve with effervescence in a bead of Na_2CO_3 ; but are insoluble in a bead of microcosmic salt $(NaNH_4HPO_4)$.

Boric Acid and Borates. $Ba(BO_2)_2$ is white.

180 (a) Alcohol added to boric acid—or a borate which has been treated with conc. H_2SO_4—and kindled, burns with a *green* flame. (b) This flame coloration is also obtained by bringing a little of the powdered borate, moistened with conc. H_2SO_4, into the Bunsen flame on a platinum wire which has first been dipped in glycerine.

Oxalic Acid and Oxalates. See Reactions 141, 148, 153.

181. (a) Heated alone, oxalic acid decomposes without blackening into CO_2, CO and H_2O ; (b) oxalates are converted, with evolution of CO and without blackening, into carbonates (cf. 174), or with evolution of CO_2 into metals. (c) Heated with conc. H_2SO_4. both the acid and its salts give off CO and CO_2 with effervescence and without blackening.

Tartaric Acid and Tartrates. See Reactions 160, 164.

182. BaTr and CaTr are readily soluble in all acids, even HAc (distinction from H_2Ox. cf. 153).

183. Solid tartaric acid and tartrates blacken when ignited and give the characteristic odor of burnt sugar.

184. Heated with conc. H_2SO_4, both acid and salts blacken and CO_2, CO and SO_2 are evolved.

185. If Ag_2Tr, precipitated from $AgNO_3$ by a neutral tartrate, is nearly dissolved by adding NH_4OH, and the solution gently heated, the test tube becomes coated with a silver mirror.

Chromic Acid, see p. 16; **Arsenic and Arsenious Acids,** see p. 12.

Sulphurous Acid and Sulphites. 186. If to a solution of barium sulphite in HCl, chlorine water is added, barium sulphate is precipitated. Sulphurous acid is a powerful reducing agent (cf. 99, 108). 187. All sulphites are decomposed by HCl with evolution of sulphur dioxide, which is recognized by its odor.

Thiosulphuric Acid and Thiosulphates. 188. Barium thiosulphate dissolves in HCl with separation of S. 189. HCl precipitates from thiosulphates, after a little, S with simultaneous evolution of sulphur dioxide.

Group II.

ACIDS WHICH ARE PRECIPITATED FROM NEUTRAL SOLUTIONS OF THEIR SALTS BY $AgNO_3$.

Sub-group A. *Acids whose Silver Salts are insoluble in* HNO_3:—HCl, HBr, HI, HCN, H_2S, ($H_4Fe(CN)_6$, $H_3Fe(CN)_6$, HClO (precipitates AgCl)).
5

Hydrochloric Acid and Chlorides. See Reactions **1, 10, 19.**

190. Most solid chlorides yield HCl when heated with conc. H_2SO_4; or Cl_2 when heated with H_2SO_4 and MnO_2.

Hydrobromic Acid and Bromides. AgBr is pale yellow; less soluble in NH_4OH than AgCl.

191. PbAc precipitates white $PbBr_2$; less soluble in H_2O than $PbCl_2$.

192. Chlorine water, added to a solution of a bromide, liberates Br_2, which colors the liquid yellow; if this solution be shaken with chloroform, ether or CS_2, the Br_2 is dissolved in it with a yellow color, which disappears on adding NaOH, or Cl_2 in excess.

193. Heated with conc. H_2SO_4, bromides yield $HBr+Br_2$; with MnO_2 and H_2SO_4, Br_2 alone.

Hydriodic Acid and Iodides. See Reactions **15, 24, 32.**

194. AgI is yellow; very difficultly soluble in NH_4OH.

195. Chlorine or bromine water sets I_2 free from iodides. The liberated I_2 colors the liquid brown, and dissolves in chloroform, ether or CS_2, forming a violet colored solution. Excess of Cl_2 produces colorless ICl_3.

196. Free iodine (cf. 195) colors starch paste deep blue.

197. Solid iodides yield violet vapors of I_2, when heated with conc. H_2SO_4 or with MnO_2 and H_2SO_4.

Hydrocyanic Acid and Cyanides. See Reactions, 46, 53, 127, 133.

198. AgCN is white, insoluble in HNO_3, soluble

with difficulty in NH_4OH ; on ignition gives Ag.

199. If to a solution of a cyanide, NaOH and small quantities of $FeSO_4$ and Fe_2Cl_6 be added, a bluish green precipitate is formed. On warming and acidifying with HCl, a precipitate of *Prussian blue* remains (cf. 96).

200. Most cyanides are decomposed by HCl or H_2SO_4 with evolution of HCN, which has the odor of bitter almonds.

Hydrosulphuric Acid and Sulphides. See
Reactions 2, 11, 20, 28, 35, 42, 49, 56, 63, 67, 73, 79.

201. Most sulphides, when treated with HCl or H_2SO_4, give H_2S, recognized by its odor and by its blackening paper moistened with PbAc.

202. All compounds containing S, when heated with Na_2CO_3 on charcoal, yield Na_2S which, when moistened, stains silver brown or black.

Hydroferrocyanic and Hydroferricyanic Acids and their Salts. See Reactions 91 and 97 ; 90 and 96. Ferrocyanide of silver is white ; ferricyanide of silver, orange. Copper ferrocyanide is brownish red ; ferricyanide, yellowish green. Boiling NaOH decomposes insoluble ferrocyanides and ferricyanides.

203. *Hypochlorous Acid and Hypochlorites* are easily decomposed by dilute acids with evolution of chlorine. Silver nitrate precipitates AgCl.

Sub-group B. *Acids whose Silver Salts are soluble in HNO_3 ;*—Group I, except H_2SO_4, HF and H_2SiF_6 ; (HNO_2).

Nitrous Acid and Nitrites. 204. Silver nitrate precipitates white silver nitrite ; soluble in acids and in a large excess of water. 205. Nitrites, both solid and in solution, are decomposed by acids with evolution of red fumes ; the acid solution decolorizes permanganate of potassium, and colors starch paste, to which KI has been added, deep blue.

Group III.

ACIDS WHICH ARE NOT PRECIPITATED BY ANY
REAGENT :—HNO_3, $HClO_3$, $CH_3.CO.OH$.

Nitric Acid and Nitrates.

205. Free HNO_3 (a) heated with Cu, gives red
fumes ; (b) boiled with fragments of quill, silk or
wool, turns them yellow.

206. HNO_3 is liberated from nitrates by conc.
H_2SO_4 and gives the tests of 205.

207. If to a solution of a nitrate, $FeSO_4$ be added
and conc. H_2SO_4 be poured carefully into the test
tube, which is inclined so that the acid runs down to
the bottom, a dark ring will appear on top of the
H_2SO_4, which will be violet, red or dark brown, according to the quantity of HNO_3 present. The ring
increases on gently shaking the tube, and disappears
on warming.

208. (a) Solid nitrates deflagrate when fused on
charcoal. (b) Heated in a glass tube, many nitrates
give red fumes.

Chloric Acid and Chlorates.

209. All chlorates are decomposed by conc. H_2SO_4
with evolution of Cl_2O_4, a greenish yellow gas of
characteristic odor. The test must be made with a
very small quantity and no heat employed, otherwise
the decomposition may take place with explosive vio-
lence.

210. (a) Solid chlorates deflagrate on charcoal.
(b) Heated in a glass tube or on platinum foil, O_2 is
evolved and a *chloride* remains.

Acetic Acid and Acetates.

211. AgNO, precipitates from not too dilute solutions white $CH_3CO.OAg$; soluble in hot H_2O and in NH_4OH.

212. Heated (a) with conc. H_2SO_4, acetates give the characteristic odor of acetic acid ; (b) with conc. H_2SO_4 and alcohol, the fragrant odor of acetic ether.

SECTION II.

EXAMINATION FOR THE ACIDS.

A systematic course of separation into groups and individuals, as in the analysis for metals, cannot be applied to the examination for acids. Their detection must be largely accomplished by the use of special tests.

Many acids are detected or indicated in the Preliminary Examination of solids and treatment with solvents. If the substance is in solution, addition of HCl to precipitate the first group may produce evidence of the presence of certain acids (cf. p. 38, g) ; others are reduced to bases by H_2S in the precipitation of the second group, and are found as metals in the regular course of analysis. If the metals which a solution contains are known, the number of acids to be looked for may be often much reduced by considering what acids may be present, and what must be absent *in solution* with the metals which have been found. (Thus, if Ba is found, we need not

5*

look for H_2SO_4.) Hence, as the examination for
metals is likely to afford much valuable information
in regard to the acids which a substance contains, the
systematic course of analysis for metals always pre-
ceeds the examination for acids.

As a general rule, all the metals except those of the
alkalies, must be removed from a solution before examining it for acids, as their presence may interfere
with the detection of some of the acids. If neither
As or Sb is present, the other metals may all be precipitated by boiling with a slight excess of Na_2CO_3.
As, Sb, as well as the other metals of Groups I and
II, may be removed by leading H_2S into the hot solution and filtering.

The solution from which the precipitated metals
have been removed by filtration is boiled with addition of HNO_3 in very slight excess, until all CO_2 is
driven off, and then exactly neutralized by adding a
slight excess of NH_4OH and warming until the solution no longer smells of NH_3 and is neutral to test
paper.

The solution thus prepared cannot contain
H_2SO_3, $H_2S_2O_3$, H_2CO_3, H_2S, $HClO$, or HNO_2.

If the original solution contains no metals or only
those of the alkalies, it is carefully neutralized, if
necessary, by means of HNO_3 and NH_4OH.

I. (a) To a portion of the neutral solution add
$BaCl_2$; a precipitate shows the presence of some one
or more of the acids of Group I.

(b) To another portion add HCl and $BaCl_2$; a
precipitate shows the presence of Group I, Sub-
group A.

If precipitates are obtained in both cases, any or all the members of the group may be present; if only in (a), Sub-group B alone is represented.

(c) Of the acids of this group the following have been found, if present, in the preliminary examination and analysis for metals:—H_2CrO_4, H_3AsO_4, H_3AsO_3 as bases; H_2SO_3, $H_2S_2O_3$, H_2CO_3, $(HO)_4Si$, HF and H_2Tr in the preliminary examination, treatment with solvents or on the addition of HCl to precipitate Group I.

The presence of the acids thus indicated must be confirmed by special tests.

II. (d) To a third portion of the neutral solution, add $AgNO_3$; a precipitate indicates the presence of some one or more of the acids of Group II.

(e) To a fourth portion add HNO_3 and $AgNO_3$; a precipitate shows the presence of Group II, Sub-group A.

If precipitates are obtained in both cases any or all the members of the group may be present; if only in (d), Sub-group A is absent. The preliminary examination and analysis for metals have given reactions for the following, if present: H_2S, HClO, HNO_2, and those common to Groups I and II given at (c). HCl, HBr, HI and HCN are also usually detected in the preliminary examination. The presence of these acids is confirmed and that of the others of the group detected by special tests.

HBr can be detected in the presence of HI, by adding chloroform and then chlorine water till the violet color disappears. If the chloroform retains a yellow color, Br_2 is present.

HCl in the presence of HBr and HI can be detected as follows :   Add $AgNO_3$ in insufficient quantity for complete precipitation **and filter.**   Repeat if necessary until the filtrate is free from Br_2 and I_2 as proved by the chloroform test.   If the filtrate then gives a precipitate with $AgNO_3$, HCl is present.

III. HNO_3, $HClO_3$ and HAc have all probably been indicated in the preliminary examination. Their presence is confirmed or detected by special tests.

EXERCISES.

XLIV. Under what condition can **Ag** and **Cl** be present in the same solution ?

XLV. A substance soluble in H_2O is found to contain **Pb, Ca** and **K** ; what acids must be absent ?

XLVI. If Cr is found in the examination for metals, how can you determine whether it was present in the original solution as a chromium salt or as a chromate ?

XLVII. A solution contains Ag and free HNO_3 ; what acids must be absent ?

XLVIII. What will be the result of mixing the following solutions :   (a) NaCl and $Pb2NO_3$;   (b) $Hg_2 2NO_3$ and $HgCl_2$; (c) $FeSO_4$ and $BaNO_3$; (d) $AgSO_4$ and $BaCl_2$?

XLIX. An insoluble compound is found to contain Ag ; how can the acid radicle be detected ?

L. How are nitrates and nitrites distinguished from each other ?

INDEX.

www.ingramcontent.com/pod-product-compliance
Lightning Source LLC
Chambersburg PA
CBHW031750090426
42739CB00008B/953